Reflections of the heart

(A collection of Poems)

Aditi Bhatpahri

NewDelhi • London

BLUEROSE PUBLISHERS
India | U.K.

Copyright © Aditi Bhatpahri 2025

All rights reserved by author. No part of this publication may be reproduced, stored in a retrieval system or transmitted in any form or by any means, electronic, mechanical, photocopying, recording or otherwise, without the prior permission of the author. Although every precaution has been taken to verify the accuracy of the information contained herein, the publisher assumes no responsibility for any errors or omissions. No liability is assumed for damages that may result from the use of information contained within.

BlueRose Publishers takes no responsibility for any damages, losses, or liabilities that may arise from the use or misuse of the information, products, or services provided in this publication.

For permissions requests or inquiries regarding this publication, please contact:

BLUEROSE PUBLISHERS
www.BlueRoseONE.com
info@bluerosepublishers.com
+91 8882 898 898
+4407342408967

ISBN: 978-93-6783-848-8

Cover Design: Aman Sharma
Typesetting: Pooja Sharma

First Edition: January 2025

www.ingramcontent.com/pod-product-compliance
Lightning Source LLC
LaVergne TN
LVHW041611070526
838199LV00052B/3101

PREFACE

Just a few days ago, I never thought I would be writing this book, but I took a writing challenge and never thought I would be able to write so many poems and compile all my work.

The past few years have been very crucial in shaping me and my life. It made me go through a lot of different experiences from which I feel I needed to learn and extract some meanings out of it. So I have just tried to put all the wisdom I gained into this book, into these poems.

Life is filled with some regrets, some realisations, some facts, some acceptance, some letting go. In time I realised life is an art of letting things go, and as we leave behind our yesterdays, our tomorrows come to our rescue. We always think in the moment that things are over; we feel this very moment to be fatal, but life goes on, and things get better, and then we wonder at the fact that how we thought just a few moments back, everything was the end of life, but it's actually just the beginning.

We get comfortable with life and its turns; we become strong. It's a book to witness the pain, its transition from brokenness to strength, to just witness the transition and how time changes everything, and for everything that we are worried about today, one day it means nothing to us. And we just move on to bigger and better problems. This is the witness of seeing oneself growing up, facing all the problems of the world. Learning to survive and becoming the better versions of ourselves. Evolving into who we are meant to be

And sometimes just accepting and witnessing the pains of life is what we need; sometimes we can't change anything, but acceptance is what sets us free.

I hold deep gratitude for this chance to write as I think this book gave me the chance to put out all my work in front of you. And I hope you all will like it too.

ACKNOWLEDGMENT

I would like to thank my parents, my dad and mom, for believing in me; my brothers, for making me believe in my own self and my capabilities; for standing tall for every dream of mine; for making me listen to my inner guidance; for making me follow my own path; and for pushing me.

To all my friends who always showed support for my writing and made me believe that this could be done, for seeing my potential and encouraging me to dream beyond my measures.

I would also like to thank the team of Blue Rose Publication for making this process so easy and guiding me in every step and through the whole process. I would also like to thank my teachers and mentors of life who imparted their wisdom throughout life.

And my followers and supporters who read my blogs and inspire me to keep on writing.

"The audacity of humans to face everything that they think will destroy them !

And yet the power and simplicity of life to survive every storm just like a normal moment passing you by ..!

You will see it slip away in just a breath .

The audacity of life to break you and yet not letting u fall ,

to make you fall but yet make you stand !

And to live and survive amidst all odds ..!!

To surpass everything that makes you feel it's never gonna be okay and yet slowly it gets away...

The power and audacity of time,

To slow down the heavy depths of pain

Till one day it's like a fleeting sound ..! "

CONTENTS

WALLS	1
WHO AM I ?	2
FIGHT	3
A CUP OF COFFEE	5
ALL WE DO IS WRITE ?	7
THE RIVER	9
ONE DAY YOU SURVIVE	10
STOP	12
TODAY	13
LIFE GOES ON !	14
DEPTHS OF SHADOWS	16
STAND	17
THE TIME WE WASTE !	18
SCARRED	26
ETERNITIES	27
WAKING UP	28
THE VOICES IN MY HEAD	31
THE PAUSE	34
THE NEW DAWN	41
A FEW THINGS UNSAID ..!	47
THE LETTERS I DIDN'T SEND	49
DREAMS	51

THE RIVER 54

LIFE IS A CANVAS 56

THOUSAND NIGHTS TO MAKE A THING STAND TALL 58

JOURNEYS 59

MOUNTAINS 60

ROSES 61

DEAR LIFE 65

THOUSAND MILES 68

उड़ान 69

सत्य 72

क्या छुपा रखा है ? 73

सच सच्चा नहीं लगता ! 75

नया सवेरा 76

यादें 77

मन्नत के धागे 78

मैं कौन हूँ ? 79

यादों की टीस 80

फासले 81

एक तूफान आने को है । 82

तुम्हारा शर्ट 83

लिखना 84

अधूरा	85
मुंबई	88
बेचैनी	89
ZINDAGI NAYI SI !	91
HUM KYA CHAHTE HAI ?	92
KYA HUM KHUSH HAI ?	93
DARK CIRCLES	95
EK ROOTHA SHAYAR..!!	96
BEECH MAJHDHAAR	98
TANHAI	99
VOH GHAR	100
ZINDAGI	104
ASAL MEIN KAUN HO TUM ??	106
WAQT	107
SILVATIEN	108
KHUDSE MOHHABAT	109
YAADEIN	112

1.
WALLS

"What did these walls see ?
That took away their voice."

If I witnessed history standing tall ,
Listening to the Secrets that goes behind it all.

I wonder, wouldn't I myself turn into a wall ?

2.

WHO AM I ?

I am Nothing, who has the Power to become everything!

I AM INFINITE.

3.

FIGHT

What is this fight of holding on & Letting go ?
For one step I take forward And
Two steps behind,

Increasing the distance,
Just By Twice.

For twice will I have to cross my feet in the same spot,
One to Fight from the fear & Once Finally standing there at all.

What is this that is making me stop from moving forward ?
I look inside and find Fear engulfing me and my heart.
Me!
Oh,
I think I found My biggest Enemy !
Finally,

For each step, I go to a war,
with an army of thousand thoughts !
Reminding me of my limitations,
Every day after the Wakeup call.

When will this fight end ?
What will put my heart to rest?
And calm the chaos and regrets !

Who will end this fight if not me ?
So I take the dagger to kill it.
And put my mind to sleep.
Because the Fight is always Me against Me !

For I win only when I defeat myself truly.
How humble life teaches us to be !
It makes you Win at the feat of Your own defeat.

And to truly live, I will have to
Let something inside me Die ..!
To let go of the one...
The Me that is holding me back,
I will have to let it go.
So that I can truly fly...!!

And I will rise like a phoenix.
From the death of my ashes
And turn to gold with a shimmering light...!
And like fire will my soul rise.
Bright,
Undefeated.
Ready to enlight...!!

4.
A CUP OF COFFEE

These Years I Survived,
And I would like to thank my Coffee !
And I am not sorry for not cutting on it.
Because it was the only warm hug that made me smile.

And yes, the best body can little wait.
As I have a double chin and a chubby face.
And the flats are gonna flat when it's time.
But yeah, this year I did survive.

And I am happy for not seeking validation.
Just for attaining the perfect shape,
Because I am happy for whoever I am.
For I don't want people to celebrate me.
After I turn into something which I will in time,
But I am ME for me at this moment itself.
And I just don't want to hate it before I say goodbye!
For I love myself in the fit size, but even when
The size of the dress increased a little by.
When did my Love depend on the scales of the size ??

And sometimes these trending reels sound stupid to me.
As if the whole of your existence has to follow certain trends.
For you to feel like you Fit in !

For I never believed myself to be fitting in.
And my soul I am unable to fix in a niche of any rhythm.

And I would like to Ask what I like !
Before I think of asking anybody what they like. ?
For something which I completely am not!
For then they love me only in parts.
For the picture I show them, of my perfect cast !!

And who loves me on days when I am not so bright ?
For I believe I want to be loved for being on that blurry side.

And I write this poem and put the last dot.
Sitting on my bed sipping coffee from the table beside,
And I put this debate aside.
I love me both Fit and Also sometimes a plus size <3

5.
ALL WE DO IS WRITE ?

Why do we write?
Is Writing enough ?

To all the horrors of the world we witness,
And all we do is Write !

How helpless we humans are!
For misery we can't change,
For fights we can't wage.
All we do is raise the voice.
And write in papers the mute outcry,
of a thousand lives !

And what lamps does it reignite ?
For the darkness of cold hearts remains untouched !
Are our efforts Futile ?

One indeed it inspires, who in turn
Turn the world to gold.
But does it ever reach down the skin of the "One,"
Who needs to change himself the most ?

Oh, Thy ignorance, and that is why I plead,
Is the strongest of all the enemies.
Because it burns the very wall of Conscience,
Which lays as the brick of the monuments,
Standing tall in the world.

And how are we going to change the world ?
If we built The Skyscrapers all resting
In a shaking ground ?

Are we deluded that it isn't all just meant to collapse ?
No matter how tall we build it and what for ?
Because everything will just collide.

And for that day I won't cry,
Because I believe the world needs some shaking and falling,
To erect the walls right this time.

Oh history, why do we repeat it every time?
Why don't we learn and erase the mistakes of the Time left behind ?
And make a better world together, standing tall after the edge of Survive.

6.
THE RIVER

A river flows in you
Take your turns
Flow and be free
And cut whatever comes in your way !

7.

ONE DAY YOU SURVIVE

And One day all your nights will turn bright.
That day might take a little long to arrive.
But One day It Will.

One day everything you are afraid of will pass you by.
And the things you thought you wouldn't be able to survive,
You will get through it and Survive.

And One fine day on a Thursday afternoon,
The hardest battle you will let go ,
And it will pass you swiftly.
Like winds slowly kissing you by.

And you will look back
And laugh at Life !
By sitting and sipping wine,
You will share these stories,
wondering the horrors you surpassed of Time !
Mocking the brutality of it, taking a Dine.

Because that is the Beauty of Time.
It changes !
No matter what kills you today,
One day you just get through it !
And Survive.

8.

STOP

And when your heart is heavy !
I hope you find the courage to stop.

I hope you catch your breath.
When life leaves you with a heavy heart.

When life chokes you by !
I hope you find strength to defeat it & rise.

What the future holds who knows ?
For a moment just let it go.

But stop you must like a pause,
So you can resume when you are strong.

For if you leave and exit now.
You will never know,
What the future will hold.
What tomorrow will bring at your door !

Learn to stop so that you don't need to quit.
Honour your stops !

9.

TODAY

Every morning gives us the opportunity to leave our yesterday behind.
To Rise after every Sunset,
To Rise after every Failure,
To Leave our shadows behind.

It gives us Hope,
Of a New beginning.
And a whole new day that is to be created.

How are you going to make Your day ?
What is it that you're gonna leave behind ?
Today ?
What are you gonna do differently today ?
How are you gonna make today's morning count ?

Because the Sun rises every day but
True morning is when "One" decides to Rise!!

So let's Rise today!!

10.

LIFE GOES ON !

Life goes on.
It always does !
And maybe this is what my heart is grieving for.
Ruthlessness of existence that maybe I can't take !
Life goes on.
And I am ready for the take.

What is life if not just a take...!!
But the one where we get a single take.
So be careful because every decision leads to a different outcome,
And leads to a world which, if we choose something else,
Where will we end ? We will never know...!

How these moments change the destiny,
God knows !
For all we can do is,
Get ready to roll...!!
And know and be cautious of what you choose.
Because each moment has the power to change the trails of the future course.
And keep in Mind while you choose,
Be free but not so free that the freedom misleads you down to your own misery!

Be clear so that you know what you stand for,
but not so rigid that you can't change your mind if you find anything wrong.
Find your rules and what you fight for ?
Otherwise, what will you and your identity stand for ?

Be not so bound by rules that you can't carve your own path !
But not so unclear that you lose the very sight and get lost.

I have come to a realisation.
A funny game of balance is life.
All you need to do is balance the high and low tides.
And stand in the ropes dancing beneath you,
your shaking ground.
And sooner you will reach the end,
walking through the edge of the knife.

11.

DEPTHS OF SHADOWS

What if the heart has found its home,
in the depths of shadows of the dark ?
What if you have seen the light in the dark?
and dark in the brightest of stars !
When Shadows have been your home for too long,
It makes you afraid of the light, not the dark...!!
Leave your shadows behind,
BreakAway...! 🕊

12.
STAND

And they ask me, Why do I have so much to say ?
And why can I never stop ?
Maybe because all my life,
I have spoken silently and survived each tragedy in silence.
Something in me just wants to shout for all the time I couldn't
And maybe fight for all the time when I wouldn't.
And so I fight every single irrelevant thing !
This anger, looming inside me.
Never stopping, never fading.
For all the times I should have but couldn't,
Stand for me...!

13.

THE TIME WE WASTE !

How much of "US" we waste on things that don't even count.
At last we regret only the things we lost as our own selves !

Because all the time we waste on things that don't matter,
Takes away and sieves away what we have left for us when,
we look back and find !

Treat time as the most precious gift.
And never gift it to the unworthy because everything comes back.
But
Not the wasted time !

And everything you can tame but not the wheels,
Of the powerful Time.
For if it slips from your hand,
your whole life you will spend in regret.
So treat it as your beloved child.
For its love and hobby is to run away from your hand,
from time to time.
Without you getting to know its vicious dance.
Never let time play such tricks on you.
So better learn to value it and who you give it to.
Because people leave one day or the other.

It's you who's left alone.
Nobody stands with you on the deserted roads.
And all the love you gave will fleet below your feet.
You will stand on the graveyard of all the love you give.
At the times of your need,
All that is lost will be you !
With nothing for you to hold.
The memories too die as the time flies,
so be careful with the whims of Time.
Don't waste it on things that do not survive!

14.

And if you can calm your mind and listen to what silence speaks,
and have the courage to lead the truth.
The answer always lies with you !

15.

"Do more of what makes your heart feel like it's at home."
Be the one who decides to go for it !!
To Run after the voice,
not heard & more often and not Silenced by
The Echoes & Voices of the world.

16.

" It was a Secret , Between Me and the Sea ..!
But I think the stars , the Moon , all knew about it
anyway !

17.

We are all stories to be told isn't it ?

18.

Let my heart bleed its sorrows in this paper.
and you be the witness that keeps these pains in your heart.
From thy pain will the flowers bloom of wisdom
And a new garden will thus be formed.

19.

And One day you look back and you look ahead,
And you find yourself right in the middle of both worlds.
And it's wonderful...!

20.

SCARRED

"Why do we fight for it even if it hurts us so Bad ?
Why do we make ourselves go through so much turmoil ?
To keep things that we know we can't have or things that we know will break us ?

Because Maybe it is beautiful even when it is scarred !

But what will I do with all these scars ?
What am I gonna do with the things that's left,
The scars that remain in my heart !!

But even then the heart cannot stop !
What is this fight of holding on and letting it all go ????
Heaven forfend my heart !

21.
ETERNITIES

It's like we all are eternity,
holding inside, the galaxies immersed in our souls.
MAYBE we are all eternities. We all infinite <3

22.

WAKING UP

I woke up today, and it felt like I had been sleeping all my life.
Living in some kind of dream.

This moment makes me question myself !

What is making me feel that,
All my life I have been asleep ?

Isn't it, Life One day, suddenly throws everything at your face
And You understand Life for the first Time.

First Time your mistakes don't matter,
Neither your past nor how did you live !
Because none of it has been lived correctly till now.
At this moment you come Face to Face,
With yourself .
And it sets you Free .
But Facing it comes with not much ease.
All our Life , We are so busy chasing something,
hating something that we did & what others did,
that we don't really live in the moment !
And the Moment passes you by.
And When you look back, it feels like so much time just went by.

With nothing left or remained.
And everything fading in.

On the other hand, this moment,
When we truly recognise,
that the beauty was always in this moment itself,
In this very breath that you take.

With tomorrow being a fleeting, far-fetching dream.
We have no clue what it might bring .
All we have is today that we can borrow.
To truly cherish.
As you Let Life unfold and let go of all the mistakes and resentments,
that you hold and let it slip down your fingers.
You Stop , You breathe ,
You realise the vastness of the existence in this very breath,
The whole world happening together at this very moment,
all just beneath your feet, just in a glimpse.
And the breath feels as long as travelling the whole world.
Sitting there in silence in a single beat.
You realise how vast life is!
And you let go of everything,
And what tomorrow is going to bring .

And finally, you realise , the Power of a moment,
of life , defeating all your sorrows.

And not let the worries take your power,
To take the beauty of this moment away from you.

You realise life is nothing else.
But this moment, the moment you breathe,
The very breath that makes you alive, with nothing else to keep !

You are not defined by anything else.
Except for the fact that you are here, alive.
Maybe then,
Maybe only then have you finally arrived and finally started living.
And finally you have woken up from your dream !

Wake up !
I hope you are finally alive.
Take a moment to pause and breathe.
You have walked a thousand miles.
Celebrate your existence.
No matter what you're going through,
One day it's all gonna be fine.
Because that is what Life is.

23.

THE VOICES IN MY HEAD

The voices in my head,
How beautiful it will be,
If these voices turn into silence instead.
With calmness and no noise.
Always swinging between power and limitations
That i am so scared.
The thought of being never enough.
And the everyday battle that does not subside.

For sometimes even the power does scare,
Because with power you don't have the luxury to fail.
With power, everyday is a battle to prove your worth,
To be standing in that exact same very point.
Maybe my heart is afraid of this everyday fight.
And that's why sometimes it loves the fall.
It's where we can breathe, we can learn, and rise.
Make mistakes. With nothing to prove
Just preparing for the greatest war.
And so yes, i confess, my soul is sometimes an imposter.
Hiding and resting behind, to escape petty fights.
So is it my fault ?

Isn't it most of the time we're lying?

To find out who can really see us standing there behind ??
And those who can see us,
We are afraid to face.
Because they know our weakness,
But also the power that we hide !
And so i wonder, why are we scared of the people?
Who can look through our souls ?
It's not easy to be looked at exactly as we are.
But why?

Why are we so afraid of our broken, vulnerable, fragile self ?
And also the power that resides ?
Never wanting to come off too weak nor too strong?
What did give us this shame to always hide??
Why we consider ourselves never good enough to appear just as we are !
And let people see beneath the facade of our crooked smile.
How i feel too much real becomes no real at all
Until we hide.

For all of us have pains inside our hearts !
So what's the point of faking the smile?
Instead of giving each other's shoulders to cry ?
Why does this thought of wearing emotions scare people off ?

Why are we so afraid that people will not take us
Just as we are !
Isn't the human race based on deception & lies?

The deeper the things,
Is always left unsaid.
Because we fear,
The insurmountable,
Beyond which our control does not lie.
And the things that does not lie in our control ,
We humans don't really it like !!

And sometimes make fools of ourselves to make people laugh at us.
And then laugh back at them for falling for our lies.
What mockery we create out of life ?
Or boast ourselves too much
To prove we are greater than the voices inside.
Why do we humans lie so much to survive ?
What fears of acceptance we have
That makes us fall for it and the ugly games of dice.

24.

THE PAUSE

How to know what is right & wrong ?
Is Right some shade of colour that we can just distinguish from far away?
Does it come with some highlights that can make it visible from 10 miles down the lane ?
Well I suppose many a time,
We really don't know what is right & wrong !
And
It mostly comes as a realisation afterwards.

Sometimes we know it in the moment itself,
So strong in the bones that we can't leave it unfelt.

But sometimes when there is no voice,
When we are sailing in an unknown territory,
Where we yet don't know,
how the moment is going to change,
the course of our destiny!
And till the time we know it's too late,
We can't turn back time and change !
All we have to do now is live with the consequences.
Oh, the heaviness of the decisions we sometimes unknowingly make .!

I think we understand right or wrong in retrospect.
Because many times,
we are not aware of the consequences a moment is going to make.
For me, right & wrong is just a lack of knowledge of the consequence.
A deck of cards, a matter of unjust fate !

But then I think, who is teaching us about this consequence?
And guiding us for life ?
Which book states and tells us what action is gonna affect you in what ways ?
And to what extent ?
Are we ever aware ??
Of all the turmoils and twists and pains ?
How do we know & calculate every action and its reaction that it creates ?
And when we do,
Oh, thy lord !
These calculations can also end up being wrong !
Heaven, never prepared us for this game....!

Makes me think life to be a Gamble.
No matter how much we think,
Not matter how much we do,
Try to run fast with time and calculate.
It's just a funny probability of even & odds,
that we can't escape !

And even if we learn , calculate, and understand
Is it ever enough ?
Because do we really ever learn ?
Until
Something happens and we face its repercussions.

We learn from experience, not from learning through books and stats.
So let life happen and flow through it.
Find guidance so that you don't slip through,
the crack of loopholes in the ocean of regret.
And even if you can't find all your answers.
Trust in your failures and rights and wrongs .!
Let the wrong guide you to your right path.
And let the wrongs fly back away in space and time.
Erase the wrongs and it's heaviness from your mind.
Because it was something that you were never prepared for...!
But learn from your false and
Try to be a better human.
Who knows and can make better decisions in the meanwhile.
So let's begin Life .

25.

Under the sheets

Under the sheets
Where heaven and hell lie.
How I wish time to stand by.
The sheets carrying the scars of our souls,
The secrets we whispered to each other.

For once I wanna hold you and
For once and for all !
Because my soul's now tired
Of letting things go.

Each story becomes unknown,
Even after reading all the pages for hours,
And people just crossing from the window,
Looking just at the covers, turning pages after pages yet knowing nothing,
What it holds, me and my soul.

Let's make our sins dance.
Because we all are sinister.
In this game of greed after all !

I never felt love so close before meeting you.
I feel you have the cure that can heal,
Me and My tainted, bleeding heart...!
I never realised something could really make me feel so warm.
The way you held me,
In your arms !
Something in me you fixed.
Just by holding me, embracing me,
in your heart.

26.

Desires kill us more than life...!!

Sometimes the deepest desires of our heart can never be fulfilled because for it to happen we have to let go of something that is maybe too essential for our existence...!!

Sometimes getting everything is not possible.

Sometimes we get what we want; sometimes we get what we need.

And sometimes maybe all we get is something that just ensures that at least we survive.!

But even if we survive, surviving with killing those wants, dreams, and needs feels no better. So basically you are stuck in a dead end, and no matter what you do, no matter how fast you run, no matter how far you go, no matter which way you choose... life will leave you miserable...!!

Maybe we expect too much from life, and truly life is not bound to make our lives good or better. It's just life, and we have to do whatever we get to the best of it! No matter what it throws at us or if it feels like the worst nightmare to us ..!!

Desires kill us more than life.
Sometimes the best we can do for ourselves is to accept Life !
Accept it just the way it is.
Save yourself from futile fights of your mind.

For whatever cards you have been dealt with, learn to deal with it.
Without blaming it and facing it,
not running away from it like a coward!
Accept your twisted fate with both arms.
Same as you would meet any triumph!
Something beautiful will come out of it.
If you learn to let go of your plans,
And surrender a bit to life's plan !

Sometimes the universe takes you in its own path !
Let go of the attachments that cause you pain.
And
Let Life Unfold !

27.

THE NEW DAWN

Sometimes Life is not as beautiful and as pleasant as it seems. No matter how hard we try, sometimes life breaks us. It breaks us in unrepairable ways. It leaves us screeching and dragging on our knees, kneeling for the mercy of the god, begging for some magic to erase everything, to turn back everything. Isn't it? Life is very unfair on some days after all.

Life, a crazy four-letter word. One day you might be at the top of the world, and just the next day your whole world could just collapse and turn into pieces. You never know! Life is really unpredictable, and you never know what the next day will bring.

There are times when it will leave you shattered, broken, crumbling. But let me tell you, these will also be the moments that will make you. As it is said, "What breaks you is also what makes you," and "It is Hardship that prepares ordinary people for extraordinary destiny."

There will be times when all you will be able to think of is how to get out of your bed. There will be nights that you will feel breathless and torn. When the pain will torment your heart and you will think you will just not be able to make it through another day.

There are times when the night seems endless. There are some days when Life seems like seeing another day would be just impossible. The days where, no matter how bright the light of your rooms is, no matter if the world is burning fireworks, your life seems just as dark as the moonless night. When there are

breaths in your body and you are alive yet it feels like your soul has died from somewhere inside.

Isn't it? Life sometimes is really Brutal ! Some days no amount of positive words can brighten up your day. Sometimes telling someone that everything will be alright is delusional ! Sometimes Hope can kill us because sometimes, no matter how hard we try, on some days we cannot find Hope. We don't have anything to look up to on some days. Those days are just long, screeching, and daunting, the never-ending nights, where every moment passes like the melting drops of snow, slow.

What should we do on those days ? Well, I can tell you a lot of things to do; I can tell you to put yourself into some other activity, some other thing, but then there will come a time when all of it will be useless, and you won't be able to delude yourself. The pain will hit you like a sharp knife. Truth will come to take your breath away, and you will not be able to do anything else. It will be like somebody is trying to kill you, and all you can do is nothing. It's like your feet are frozen, and you cannot move; you cannot do anything to dodge the knife.

Isn't it? Life hits us like this only. And what are we able to do ? Did we see it coming? No. Could we do anything to stop it ? No ! Isn't it Life makes us understand how powerless we are in front of it? We can do nothing. If it's gonna hit you, it's gonna ! So better take it.

Take it with courage, take it with pride, take it with tears in your eyes. Because this is what it is to be human. The only thing that you must remember on those nights is it's all about Time.

And Time has a habit of changing, and it does change. I know that at such times you cannot make yourself feel better with any

words, or you don't have any explanation or last hope to cling to. Everything seems black, but it will pass. It is bound to pass. Just hold on there; let it be, be with it, let it choke you, keep on gasping; it will pass.

There are a lot of things in this world listening to which our soul shakes. Which makes us give up on every strength of life we have. But what can we do? All we can do is fight it to the best of our power. Rise above it; let it be in the past. There are moments in life that shake your whole existence. Be it simply the thought of losing someone, the betrayal of your loved one, or any big tragedy. Some things leave us numb; some things just kill us from within. It feels like we are living, but deep down we can't feel anything, neither happiness nor anything.

I will not say that any of such things will never happen in your Life but I hope not. It is life, and it is bound to break you, shape you, and do whatever it wishes to. But all I want here is for you to understand that no matter what happens to you, You can Rise above it. It may seem impossible. It may be impossible to even think of a new beginning or a new morning. But don't give up; just hold on. I will not say it will be dawn... Sometimes there is no dawn, just darkness. But no matter what, hold on and never give up. If you are someone who has gone through something really bad, and no matter how small it is for the world, if it is something that broke you, and if it is the reason why you walk in those streets lost and empty, thinking that life is an unlimited chain of sorrow and injustice, I hope you understand that one day, it will all be okay. I don't know how long it will take for you to come back to yourself. I don't know how long the cut's life has given you or how long it will take for it to heal.

I don't know if it will ever be able to give you back everything you lost.

But that is the beauty of Life . You never know what the next moment brings. It may seem like an endless night, but what if a beautiful dawn is waiting for you? It is taking a long time, and I know it's getting unbearable, but life is uncertain, and you have no clue if life has so much in store for you just after a few miles.

That is the beauty of probability; it gives you hope even when everything seems fatal.

Hope is an absurdity sometimes that can shape into reality however impossible it seems.

So my dear friend, I hope this is the voice you need to hear to give you the strength to believe that you will find you. Life will blossom again.

But you don't give up. I don't want you to give up. I don't want you to be lost in the faded thoughts of the past. I want you to shine like a bright early morning. I want you to make everybody believe in the power of the dawn. That yes, Life is What You make. And no matter how many setbacks you face, Your Life is not the definition of your limitations; instead, it is fuelled by those limitations to make you more fearless, more powerful, unstoppable, and limitless. You matter. You are priceless, and I want you to wake up for you. I want you to look into the eyes of those chains that hold you and tell them that it won't be able to hold you back anymore. Come what may! It will never be able to stop you. And I am not telling all this out of the blue just to say. I know positivity seems stupid and fake on some days. And it makes us feel like one cannot see us in our shoes. I know saying all this is easy, but I am not saying it just for the sake of saying

it. I am saying it because I know how daunting it feels to be at such a place. It feels like it will never end. It feels like Your Life is another name for misery. No matter how hard you try, life just puts you back on the ground. And it feels terrible. I am telling all this because I have seen people who have been in such places, which made them give up on the beauty of life and their happiness because of some very shocking life experience.

I won't say everything will change. All I assure you is, if you try to change and just give life another chance, give hope another chance to make a house in those burnt bridges. I tell you, "You will be whole again ! Your home will bloom." And this time you will grow into a much wiser, much taller, much beautiful, much stronger house. I want you all to give life another chance, no matter how brutally it has killed you amid living. I want you all to smile again despite the pains life throws at you. Because you deserve it. We all deserve it. We all deserve to bloom into our most beautiful version, to live life to the fullest, and to shine again.

I hope this gives you the strength to create your new life. And I don't care how many times life has failed you; that's on it, not you, no matter how many times you have failed on your own self. No matter how many times it has bled you. I want you to Rise even after it all. Wearing those bloodshed and scars as your badge of honour to tell the world your story. Because it's you who has been given this opportunity to walk in the fire and tame the beast of life with your own bleeding hands. And I would like to tell you,

Not everybody gets to tell the story of a warrior's heart!

You will Rise Again .
You will Feel Again .
You will Smile Again.

" Awaiting , The New Dawn ."

28.

A FEW THINGS UNSAID ..!

And sometimes all I really wish !
Is that nothing could lie between us...
Time and spaces far apart, but still you could hear me in spite of all.
All the silence you could get,
And all the things I left unsaid...
This silence between us,
All I wish is that this silence in me could be heard.
And your voices didn't go unheard.
And in my eyes you could see,
Everything! That I hide beneath.
Or maybe you just could know,
Whatever I could not speak.
And there you would be sitting with me,
Watching those lovely skies, knowing whatever there is in my mind.
And not a word we both would utter.
We would talk in silence ...
And listen to what our hearts stutter.
Few things left unsaid...
Maybe someday you would know...!

Maybe someday you would know,

Few things that I left unsaid !
And just left, without letting you know.

29.
THE LETTERS I DIDN'T SEND .

Beyond all the eternities, your soul rests at the laps of peace.
So I will ask you ...
Will you be my peace ?
Because everything else leaves.
And so then I myself quietly leave,
Because
Maybe I am afraid that in you, I may find my peace.

Should I not be afraid?
What if it's not, and it just seems ?
What if peace comes at the cost of disruption later ?
Shall I take peace ? Or leave and go .?

But then where shall I go...?
Because here is where my soul rests.
This feels so peaceful; I really don't wanna go !
And so I leave all worries and let thoughts pass by.
And watched you fall asleep, sitting beside .

Some moments, how I wish we could just stop them.
The moments where everything flows,
just like the music and the feathers dancing,
on the tunes of the breezy air,
making me feel like I am grooving with them as well !

Existing feels good in this very moment,
beside you,
like a feather... light, beautiful, soft
as if my soul found a shoulder to rely on.
I don't know how to describe the bliss I am feeling right now.

I hope we all find this bliss.
And the heart we all can call our home.

30.

DREAMS

*What is even life without Dreams ? Dreams that make your life worth living. Dreams that make you wake up every morning with hopes in your hearts, that make your heart jump up at the sound of your alarm. It's truly said, " **DREAM GIVES US THE WINGS WE NEED TO FLY**." Dreams are the colours that paint up the skies of our lives. Without dreams, our life would be just mere existence, isn't it?*

Well, a question strikes my head ! What are our dreams made up of ? What is the thing that drives it ? Is it our inner sub consciousness that leads to it ?? How are our Dreams formed? Isn't it something deeply intertwined with our existence, our own self ? Something that is very innate, very close to our hearts.

But is having a Dream enough ? Is that all it takes ? Well, not at all !

In a world full of billions of people with billions of Dreams , is only having a Dream enough ?What is the thing that separates one from all ? We all are on the journey to live the dreams of our life, to make it a reality , which we can touch, which we can feel.

There are millions of eyes that shine because of the light of their dreams. We all are in the way trying our best to shape it, but is this enough? And what is enough? Who is going to tell us ?

Isn't it we all wonder what if's and the probability of life ? Will it ever come true, we ask ourselves, looking at the mirror when

no one's watching us through the hall ? Every morning with the rising sun also rises the fear, the fear of failure and the ifs and if nots.

But when has it ever stopped the Dreamer?

" The Dreamers , as the world considers them crazy, maybe because a bit they are, but it is what sets them apart."

And here they are, chasing a yet-to-be-seemingly impossible dream. Amid the destiny and trials of failures and everyday life war. A Dream that only they can see. For every Dreamer, wakes up with a longing to reach where he desires, sometimes a thousand feet apart. But every journey starts with a step. Have faith you will reach there, and this for sure.

And even if you fail, Never let it crumble you. Because whatever the Destiny be , you will always end up where you are meant to be. If you look closely, you will find yourself in every dreamer, because we all are made of the same dreams, each different in their own ways. We all are trying to chase it, and one day we all will get closer to the Destiny that awaits.

I hope if you are someone who is on the journey to create their life, this may be the strength you need to go forward. Because we all need strength to keep pushing. I hope these words connect to you and help you and soothe you because I see you; I see you behind those closed doors, working day in and day out. This is to assure you that your efforts will not go in vain. This is to celebrate the strength of people like you, who go out wearing odds on your shoulders to create the things that are not that easy and require you to risk it all. One day everything will be worth whatever you endured. Just hold on.

Your future awaits you !

As it is said, Ambition is the path to success; persistence is the vehicle you arrive in. Keep persisting till you arrive, because The future also awaits you after all !

Keep Walking…. !!

31.

THE RIVER

I sat beside the river...!
The river asked me,
What was I lamenting for ?
I told it with a sigh,
All about my worries,
And things that bother my heart !
The river told me,
"Why do you keep something that has already passed?"

I realised Life is like a River .
All the things just flow,
And never stops.
So why bother about a moment ?
That has happened in the past.
Or has never happened at all ?

I left my worries and my past behind.
And the river flowing took it away somewhere far.
What a beautiful way to create a beautiful new start!
Each moment gives us the opportunity to be new,
And to leave everything that bothers us behind.

So I left the "me" that ever came in my way,
To create a ME that is the best ever come so far...!
And bid adieu and thanked the ME I left,
Because that's who has brought me till here this far !
And here we are, ready for our fresh start !

32.
LIFE IS A CANVAS

Isn't life like a blank canvas ?? We each have our own and it all depends on us how we paint it !

And it scares us isn't it ?

What are we even supposed to paint in it ?

Will it ever be good enough ?

Will we ever be able to paint it in the way we want it to be and create a life of our dreams the way we wish it to be ?

And a lot of fears and questions that come just by staring into a blank space !

Makes me question .. Is blank space ever blank enough ?

Or is it filled with anything and everything possible .

And this made me wonder .. Why do we gaze at those skies ?

Isn't it also just another blank space ?

But is it really blank ?

Or is it filled with dreams , thoughts and questions of each one of us , when we look into those skies ?

Well I suppose it's our wishes that draws us to the skies ..! Listen to it .. listen to the inner voice and what it's trying to say to you .

How are we gonna paint it , we will only get to know once we start to paint it with our own colours .

I hope you create the most beautiful painting on the canvas of your life ..!

And never ask anybody to tell you how they like your painting, because it is solely yours.

Fill it with your own colours, in your own ways and love it for whatever it is!

Because you have created it.

Let yourself paint your own masterpiece out of life.

Lots of love ♡

33.

THOUSAND NIGHTS TO MAKE A THING STAND TALL

It takes thousands of nights and days to create something,
And make a thing stand tall.
And all it takes is mere seconds for it to fall.
But when you are picking the whole fallen pieces to create it again ..!! Remember to hold on to the courage !
It won't stand again on a single day itself.
But I'll tell you.
One day, It will !
Just hold on for a bit long.

34.

JOURNEYS

Is the person ever aware, where the journey would ever take him?
I think no. He never is !
He simply aims to reach a certain point.
And so he starts walking to reach there.
How the roads are going to mould the way of the person,
And where will he reach ?
Only the journey will tell.
Because unlike the road journeys,
where we are certain of the destination,
Life's journey is never supposed to be like it... I suppose !
Happy journey, People...!!

May you find the answers you are looking for.
May the wind take you to the place where you intend to be.
May the roads find you.
May all your soon turn to finally !
And you recognise all the silent whispers,
That the Universe is trying to speak to you .
May it all start making sense soon.
And you reach where you want to reach.
Where Life wants you to reach .... !!!

35.

MOUNTAINS

The mountains shouted a name !
And here I follow the trail.
The sounds echo the voice of my heart.
And I can never be so beautifully lost.
I hope you find the courage to follow,
where the voice of your heart leads !

36.

ROSES

As the sun peeps through the windows,
All the Red Bloomed.
With each petal carrying the written stories of beloved's heart,
No wonder why it is chosen to say silent whispers of
Lovers adorn !
A secret of a lover whispered to the rose,
It's the secret it carries, which spreads its fragrance,
And makes it bloom.

37.

I want to be saved, but I don't want to be saved.
Because maybe I am the one who drowned me !
I wanna rise on my own, but still I want someone to be by my side.
I want to be heard; still, I want to be away from all the noise.
It's a paradox, isn't it, life?
Maybe I drowned my voices to listen to yours.
Or maybe I was sad because even while speaking, I felt my voice wasn't listened to at all.
Maybe that's why I escape.
Because I feel the need to be heard.
How strange is it ?
There can be 1000 people who listened to you but no one really heard. It gives my heart a pain so heavy, the pain of being completely unheard.
No matter how much I shout or say whatever in the top of my voice, it seems somebody has muted me, and nobody can really comprehend what it really feels like or what I say!
Isn't it ? The world is as crazy as this and as this sounds ?
I don't wanna speak out loudly because I don't wanna feel unheard.
I don't wanna keep quiet because I don't wanna feel like
I am keeping it all inside.
Makes me think,

What was I supposed to do at that time !
" that time "
And if I get a chance, I will go back to that time and save myself this time.
But I don't know what would have saved me.
Because only if it was that easy and did I know how
I would have really saved me !
Maybe I was destined to drown.
I will get up again.
I know !
But what will happen if one day my heart realises it's you because of whom I drowned?
Or maybe it already knows.
How is it to accept it?
And will it let it all go?
How will everything ever be okay again ?
It seems everything is broken into pieces,
I wanna keep the pieces forever in my heart.
I wanna hold on even when it hurts, even when it bleeds. I don't wanna throw it away, like nothing happened between us ever at all.
But no matter how hard I try to forget the scars,
It bleeds me!
And reminds me how I can't walk again unless I leave it behind and move forward once and for all.

I wrote this poem because when we are young, we value everything so much. And some things that we hold too close to our heart that we never want to lose, we try so much to keep it with ourselves even when it is the same thing that causes us pain. But we don't want to let it go. It is very hard, I know. But sometimes the cure is in the pain, and the only good you can do for yourself, to set away the pain is to just let things go! I know it's hard, but that's the truth, which we need to accept. And face and accept the sorrows of our life with open arms. It is what will set us free from all attachments that weigh us down and stop us from living free and happy.

Most of the time we ourselves are the barriers that we have to fight against to set ourselves free.

38.

DEAR LIFE

I don't know what you want from me.
But sometimes I feel nothing is working out.
And I know one needs to have Patience.
But every once in a while all I question is,
Am I on the Right path ?
Somedays these paths just make me Question
my own Sanity, every moment !
Like Something I am not able to Fight.
Somedays its like I am in the middle,
of this long deserted lands,
where nothing is making Sense
with no clue how will I go Ahead !
And then I run to find Answers,
In hope to Listen from somebody
Something that can make me Believe
that Maybe I Belong !
to remove all this restlessness,
But then I think why do we always have to run
and listen from Somebody else ?
How can Somebody Else decide our FATE, our DESTINY
our LIFE ?
when did we became Slaves to other People's Perception

and gave somebody else the Power & Control
of our lives .
I Rise , Awake & Ignite.

39.

In the plethora of things that one must not forget, human beings always end up forgetting the things not to be forgotten and never forget the things that must be forgotten!

40.

THOUSAND MILES

At last,
What do we have to offer otherwise ?
If not the truth and our courageous hearts.
I feel ... I fear...!
Because the distance between my feet seems like miles a second,
and there as it is, the second forth !
Am I deluded ?
Or is this a dream ?
Or have I lost my senses?
Because my mind deceives ?
How can I stand in the same place yet it feels like miles apart ?

" Kabhi kabhi do kadmon ke beech ki doori kai mile hoti hai !
Hum chalte hai ek kadam par dekho toh aisa lagta hai
Jaise us ek kadam chalne ke liye mano kai milon ka rasta tay kar ke aaye ho ! "

1.

उड़ान

" न लिखना तुम मेरे रंग रूप और चाल के बारे में "
लिखना तो तुम लिखना मेरे उड़ान के बारे में
यूँ सींचा है अपने ख़ून से अपनी उड़ान को मैंने
ना बाँधना तुम इस उड़ान को किसी दायरे में
भूल चुक की माफ़ी
अभी तो चलना शुरू किया है
आसमान है अभी बाकी !

2.

उलफ़त में खोये रहने दो तुम्हारे
होश में सब बिखरा सा लगता है !

3.

यूँ रेत की तरह ही मयस्सर नहीं तुम
जितना पाना चाहो हाथ से छूट ही जाते हो !

4.

सत्य

क्या सत्य है और क्या झूठ,
कौन अपना और कौन पराया।
ये सब पल पल में बदले,
यही है दुनिया की माया।
ये सच को पहनाता है झूठ का लिबास
और नचाता है उसे कोर्ट के कोठे में दे हिसाब !
बोली लगती है यहाँ बेचने सच को
और बिक जाता है , सच कौड़ियों के दाम।
और दुनिया चलती है उस कौड़ी से ही,
करके अपनी आँखें बंद, ख़रीद काले चश्मे भरे धूप बाज़ार !
सच, सच बोले, कर ले प्रयत्न हज़ार
पर रंग जाता है झूठे अख़बारों की ख़बर के रंगों से हर बार।
और झूठ उठाके चलता है बिना शरम,
ख़रीद के गवाहों को और सियासी अख़बारों को बोले दाम।

5.
क्या छुपा रखा है ?

क्या कहती है ये तस्वीरें ना जाने
क्या कहते हैं ये दीवार
क्या है जो छुपा रखा है
हवाओं ने इन सरसराते टहनियों के मजधार !!!
ये गीत ये गुनगुनाहट
ये पायलों की झनकार
समय और उसकी ये चाल !!!

6.

जिनके मंसूबे बुलंद होते हैं
वो लन्तरानी में वक़्त ज़ाया नहीं करते,
जिनके इरादे हो आसमान के
वो तूफ़ानों से घबराया नहीं करते।

7.
सच सच्चा नहीं लगता !

झूठ को सच मानने की हमें इतनी आदत सी हो जाती है कि
सच कह दे कोई जो
तो वो सच सच्चा नहीं लगता !
झूठ की इतनी आदत है हमें कि
सच में झूठ ना हो तो सच अच्छा नहीं लगता !

8.
नया सवेरा

दिल ए दाग़दार हो चुका है पद शिक़श्ते फ़ाश से
डर सा लगता है फ़ीज़मानिना हालात से
अशुफ़्तगी में ढल सी गई शाम है
टूटी उम्मीदों से हिल चुकी
सपनों के पायदार मकान है
पर नया सवेरा आने को है।
एक नई जीत लाने को है।

9.
यादें

तुम्हें पिरोया है मैंने इन धागों में
इन रंगों में, इन वादों में
तुम्हें ओढ़ा है मैंने इन लाल और नीले धागों में
इन गहनों में, इन यादों में !
तुम उस गजरे की महक और मेरे श्रृंगार हो
तुम इन होठों की हया भी और मुस्कान हो
तुम हो इनमें और मुझमें समाये हुए
तुम्हें भूलू भी तो कैसे मैं ?
तुम हो मुझमें ही समाए हुए।
तुम्हें चाहा है इस बेतरतीबी से मैंने
तुम हो मेरे हर रोम में समाए हुए ॥

10.
मन्नत के धागे

उन मन्नतों के धागों का क्या करेंगे हम
जो बांध आये थे तुम्हारी चौखट में।
यूँ मांगने में तो इतना विश्वास रखते नहीं थे
ये क्या बना दिया इश्क़ ने हमें तुम्हारे।
तेरे चौखट पर आऊँ मैं हर वक़्त
ख्वाहिशों के सजदे लिए
ये भी भला कोई बात है ?
अच्छा ही किया, पूरा नहीं किया !
इंसान को हर चीज़ मिले ये भी कोई बात है !
बहुत लड़ ली तुमसे मैं, इन ख्वाहिशों के फ़सानों में
अब क़बूल कर लिया है, ख़ुशी तुम्हारे हर इरादे में।

11.
मैं कौन हूँ ?

मैं वास्तव में कौन हूँ

मैं जितना इस प्रश्न के तरफ खुद को बढ़ते जाते देखती हूँ ,

उतना ही मैं और उलझ जाती हूँ

ये समझने में कि मैं कौन हूँ ?

मैं वो हूँ ..

जो मैं दिखाती हूँ या वो हूँ जो मैं छुपती हूँ ?

कभी कभार ..इन दोनों का फ़र्क मैं समझ नहीं पाती !!

असल में कौन है हम ,

ये क्या आप जानते हो ?

मैं तो नहीं जानती !

12.
यादों की टीस

कल यादों की टीस उठी थी
आज नफ़रतों का सैलाब आएगा ।
ये कैसी सज़ा देती हूँ तुमको
कि सजा ही नहीं देती ।
ऐसी तो नहीं थी मैं
मैं यूँ रुकने वालों में से नहीं हूँ
तुम कब समझोगे ।
बेवकूफ़ हूँ मैं, अब भी तुम्हें समझाना चाह रही हूँ
ना तुम तब समझे थे , ना अब समझोगे ।
बेफ़ज़ूल मैं कब से ये तराने गाए जा रही हूँ
जाओ अब तो समझ भी जाओगे,जो तुम कभी
तो भी ये दिल माफ कर सकेगा न तुम्हें कभी
ये सज़ा तुम्हारी है या मेरी मुझे समझ नहीं आता ।
ख़ैर छोड़ो, जाओ ,तुम्हें वैसे भी कुछ समझ नहीं आता !

13.
फासले

हमें बदनाम ही रहने दो
उस शोर में धड़कनों की आवाज़ ज़रा धीरे ही सुनायी पड़ती है।
वो मिले तो उसे कहना बहुत ख़ुश है हम,
फ़ासलों का शोर बेवफ़ाओं को कहाँ सुनाई देती है।
कभी-कभी फासले देने पड़ते हैं
जब हौसला ख़ुद फासले तय करने के न हो
कभी कभार फासले मिल जाते हैं
फिर बात चाहे उम्र भर साथ चलने का ही क्यों न हो।

14.
एक तूफान आने को है ।

एक समुंदर दफ़न है मेरे सीने में कहीं
कई राज़ तैरते हैं उसमें यूँही कहीं ।
सीने का ये भार कहीं लिख दूँ तो
डर है किनारों को डूबा ना दे
तूफ़ान से उठे ये सैलाब कहीं ।
खामोश है, अभी वक्त के सन्नाटों की तरह
कोई भी पत्थर फेंके चाहे कितने ज़ोर से
समुन्दर में डूब ही जाता है ।
ये दर्द भी सीने में कहीं
डूब ही जाता है ।
डर है क़यामत की रात आने को है
डर है एक तूफान कहीं आने को है
उजाड़ के पुरानी दुनिया
एक नया बसेरा आने को है ।
ऐ दिल तू थम जा
एक नया सवेरा आने को है ।
ऐ दिल तू थम जा
एक तूफ़ान कहीं आने को है ।

15.
तुम्हारा शर्ट

परसो तुम्हारा पुराना शर्ट मिला, जो तुमने मुझे दे दिया था !

मैंने उसे देखा तो मुझे एहसास हुआ कि मैं कितना आगे आ गई हूँ ज़िंदगी में। अब उसको देख मानो कुछ नहीं लगता, बस शायद याद आता है कि हाँ ये सब पीछे छोड़ आई हूँ। न मुस्कान थी न कोई शिकन, बस एहसास वक्त के बीतने का !

अब पुरानी यादों को गले से लगाने का मन नहीं करता।

सच में बहुत दूर आ गई हूँ मैं।

16.
लिखना

लिखना मेरे लिए कभी आसान नहीं था, बस शायद आदत।

इसीलिये जो भी मेरे मन में आता है, मैं हूबहू उसे उतार देती हूँ।

पर कभी-कभी मैं ये सोचती हूँ कि जीवन के विषमताओं को सरलता से इन पन्नों में उतारना आसान है क्या या इन विषमताओं को समझना ?

क्योंकि आपकी लिखावट आपके स्पष्टता पर ही निर्भर करती है।

सोच सही हो तो लिखावट भी अच्छी हो जाती है।

मुझे लगता है जब हम लिखते हैं तो अपने भीतर झांकते हैं! हम अपने आप से मिलते हैं। अपनी गहराइयों को जान पाते हैं।

हमें अपने होने का एक वजूद मिलता है,

हमारी सोच मिलती है।

हमारी पहचान !

हमारी सोच ही हमारी पहचान होती है आख़िर।

अपने विचारों को जान के एक स्थायित्व मिलता है !

और उस वक़्त हम पूर्ण होते हैं!

क्योंकि हम ख़ुद से मिल जाते हैं।

17.
अधूरा

जब कोई चीज़ अधूरी छूट जाती है...
तो पता नहीं मुझे ये समझ नहीं आता, वो किसकी होती है ..?
क्या वो अधूरी हमारी होती है या उसके अधूरे रहने के साथ-साथ उसका अस्तित्व मिट जाता है ?
अधूरा होने और न होने में क्या कोई अंतर नहीं ?

इसलिए जो चीज़ पूरी हो सके और जिसे तुम पूरा कर सको उसका ही महत्व है।

पर अधूरा पूर्ण न होकर भी पूरे रूप से अधूरा नहीं होता !
उसमें होता है तप, उसके अधूरे रह जाने का मलाल,
उसे पूरा बनाने का प्रयास !
उसके अधूरे छूट जाने की याद।

तो इस प्रकार अधूरा रह जाना अपने आप में कुछ है।
और न होना नहीं है।
अधूरा भी अपने अधूरेपन में पूरा है, पूर्ण है अपने अधूरेपन में !

18.

कभी कभी मुझे ऐसा लगता है जैसे न जाने क्यों लिखना इतना सरल है, फिर भी मुश्किल !

मैं कोई चीज़ सोचती हूँ, पर मैं जब लिखने बैठती हूँ मानो सब जैसे मिट जाता है।

मैं जैसे ही कलम उठाती हूँ कुछ लिखने, मैं ये भूल जाती हूँ कि उस कलम को आगे बढ़ाऊँ कैसे ?

मैं कोई कहानी गढ़ नहीं पाती और उसे अधूरा छोड़ आगे बढ़ जाती हूँ।
और ये सोच में पड़ जाती हूँ कि आगे लिखूँ क्या ?

अभी मैं अपने मन की सारी बातों को बिना सजाए बिना किसी सजावट और बिना बदले
साफ लिख रही हूँ। कभी-कभार उसे प्रकट कर पाती हूँ,
और कभी कभार नहीं।
कभी-कभार अपने ख़्यालों में खोके मैं उन्हें कोई सच्चा रूप और सही शब्दों में बाँध नहीं पाती।
पर लिखती जरूर हूँ।

शायद लिखना हमेशा से ही बेहद पसंद है मुझे।

शायद सीधा सरल लिखना ही असल में लिखना है !
और जो मिलावट करते चले जाते हैं वो लिखने से उतना ही दूर चले जाते हैं।

और कभी-कभी मैं सोचती हूँ क्या मैं कभी लिख पाऊंगी जो भी मैं लिखना चाहती हूँ ?

फ़िलहाल क्या लिखना चाहती हूँ ये तो मालूम नहीं !

उसे जानने और पहचानने के लिए मुझे उस शून्य, अपनी समझ, अपनी वास्तविकता को जानना और पहचानना पड़ेगा।

तो शुरू करते हैं खुदकी तलाश।

और लिखते-लिखते मैं पहुंच ही जाऊंगी खुद तक,

और मिल ही जाऊँगी खुदसे।

19.
मुंबई

मुझे लगता है ये शहर एक आग की भट्ठी है! शहर में हर कोई अपने आप को कोयला सा तपाता है,जलाता है ताकी वो हीरा बन सके। कुछ निखर जाते हैं कुछ टूट जाते हैं और कुछ इस कुछ बनने के दौड़ में खुदको बहुत पीछे छोड़ आते हैं! ये आपको कठोर भी बना देता है और काफ़ी विनम्र भी। ये आपको सच्चाइयों से वाकिफ कराता है और सच्चाई तारों की तरह चमकदार नहीं होती, बल्कि अँधेरों से भरी होती है । पर इस शहर की हवा में एक जादू है क्योंकि कुछ बनने और पाने से दूर यहाँ हर शक्स अपने सपनों को जीने के लिए संघर्ष करता है।

जो ख़ुद उसे अपने आप मे जीना सिखाती है और जिंदगी से प्यार करना सिखाती है ! बिना कुछ पाने और खोने के शर्तों के ।

20.
बेचैनी

आँखें न जाने क्या ढूंढती हैं ...
अजीब सी एक बेचैनी है मेरे अंदर,
जो ख़त्म ही नहीं होती है

सोती हूँ तो सोने नहीं देती !
किस चीज़ की तलाश है ?
कोई ज़िक्र भी नहीं छेड़ती ।

बस एक आवाज़ है
जिसके पीछे मैं भाग चली हूँ
जाना कहा है ?
वो पता भी नहीं पता..!
अजीब सी आवाज़ है जो कहीं थमने ही नहीं देती..!

बस ऐसा लगता है जैसे
किसी चीज़ की तलाश है ।
और वो चेहरा अंजान है
हर दरवाज़ा खटखटाती हूँ
और लौट जाती हूँ निराश !

कहाँ है ये रास्ते ?
और कहाँ ले चले हैं ये मुझे ?
मंज़िलों पर पहुँच कर पूछूँगी एक दिन उन्हें..!

मिलेगी कि नहीं मंजिल.. ?
ये मुसाफिर कभी सोचते हैं क्या !
ये प्रश्न पथिक के पांव कभी रोकते हैं क्या ?

बेचैनी है इस बात की कि पता नहीं क्या ढूंढने चली हूँ ?
बस थमते नहीं ये पैर, जब तक मिल न लूं उससे एक बार !

अजीब सी ये बेचैनी है न जाने होगी कब दूर ?
सवाल जो सताता है वो बस यहीं की
पहचानूँगी कैसे मंजिल को ?
क्योंकि कोई तस्वीर कहाँ है मेरे पास !

हम सब रास्तों पर चल पड़ते हैं
कहाँ ले जाए ये हमें …?
कहां पता है हमें ये बात..!

फिर भी चल पड़े हैं इन रास्तों में
मिलके रहेंगे मंजिल से,
जो भी हो इस बार..!

1.
ZINDAGI NAYI SI !

Zindagi ek naye panne ki tarah lagne lagi hai .
Jaise kisi baarish ne sara dard nikal feka ho .
Aur ek kora panna mil gya ho !
Aise lagne laga hai jaise zindagi ki ek nayi shuruwat hai

Aur kisi toofan ne har wo cheez tabah kar di ho
Jo mujhe tabah kar rhi thi kahi

Har toofan bura bhi nhi hota shayad
Kuch naya basera lane ke liye bhi hota hai !

2.

HUM KYA CHAHTE HAI ?

Vaise toh hum sab jaante hai ki hum kya chahte hain !
Hazaaron khwahishien ,dil me kahi na kahi jhankti hai .
Par phir bhi mai sochti hu ..
Kya hum sach me jaante hai ,
Ki hum kya chahte hai ?
Aur kya hum jo chahte hain ,
Kya woh hum sachme chahte hai ?

3.

KYA HUM KHUSH HAI ?

Kya hum sach mein khush hai ?
Ya bass duniya ke is khush dikhne ke natak me kahi ghum hai ?

Kya hum sachme aazad hai ?
Ya zindagi ke pahiyo ke hisaab se chal rahe hai bass .

Kyu hum ladd rahe hai ? Kabhi khud se ,
Kabhi duniya se ?

Kyu kabhi saara jahan apna lagta hai
Aur phir vahi paraaya ?

Kyun likh rahi hu mai ye baatein ?
Bass Samajh sakun khud ko thoda issi bahane !

4.

Likhna kyu hi zruri hai ?
Ya sab baaton ko batana ?
Sab kuch batayenge sab kuch haasil hojaane ke baad !
Ye raston ke musafiro ki kahaniya bhi bhala koi sunta hai kya ??

5.

DARK CIRCLES

I love my dark circles !

" ye nishani hai un hazaar Jangho ki jinse mai ladi hu .
kabhi jeeti hu kabhi hari hu !!
zindagi se maine ye sikha hai ki ladna apne aap me hi
khud Jeet se badi ek Jeet hai ..
zindagi mein maine ye sikha hai ki zindagi ..
Jeet aur haar se pare ek Jeet hai ..! "

6.

EK ROOTHA SHAYAR..!!

Kuch toh rutha hai mere ander
Kuch toh chuta hai mere ander

Zindagi lagti hai Jeet ki ek haar
Ye haar ajeeb si lagti hai
Jaise yun na jaane kyun hi kiya ho
Itni koshish , jab tutna hi tha
Toh jodne aur banane ka prayas

Shayad ek malal hai dil me kahin
Yun jo Jeet ke bhi jeet hamari nahi huyi

Nafrat si hoti hai koshisho se mujhe
Jo mere hath kuch aaya hi nahi
Aaya toh aaya
Sirf Apmaan ..!!

Har koshish ki subah ki sundar shaam nhi hoti
Aasman me taare na chamke tab Tak raat nhi hoti

Yun suna aangan aur galiyare bhi aate hai
Kabhi haath me jaise inaam

Kabhi suni reh jaati hai voh hi rooh
Jiske kavitaaon me taliya bajati hai
Puri duniya Kai baar ..!

7.

BEECH MAJHDHAAR

Zindagi se Bhaag rahi hu shayad kahi mai
Sab aise bikhar gaya hai !
Socha tha kya banane ka
Aur na jaane kya ban gaya hai
Toota bikhara faila huya
Khudka aksh bhi dhundla sa ..!
Toote devar aur toote aayine
Khudko bhi insaan aise me kaise hi pehchaane?
Kya har cheez khud ke chahne se ho jaati hai ?
Ya duniya chalti hai apni hi koi chaal !
Le leti hai zindagi apne shatranj me harake
Ek ajeeb sa koi rukh Kai baar
Na jaane beech mein phas jaati hai
Zindagi ki naav beech majhdhaar
Yun ant me pahunch ke na jaane kya hoga
Abhi toh phasse hai beecho beech is raah

8.

TANHAI 🍃

Kya tanhaiyon ka Sabab Laya hai
Tu bhala yaha kisse Milne aaya hai ?

Bhala banjar zameen me fasal lautti hai kya ?
Yeh kaisa aaas tune failaya hai !

9.

VOH GHAR

Na Jane kitne ghar hai jinhe mai peeche chod aayi hu
Mai musafir hu ,
Tumko apne dil ka Raaz bataayi hun !

Dukh is baat ka hai ki …
unki gali se jab bhi nikale..
Woh kabhi baahon mein bharne nahi aaye !
Voh Hume rokne Nahi aaye !

Is bheed me bhut akela mehsoos krti hu khudko,
Jo hum gye ..
woh Humse Milne nahi aaye !

Voh Hume kabhi baahon mein bharne nahi aaye !

10.

Tumhe rakh liya hai maine , ek raaz ki tarah !
Khamoshiyon me doobe alfaz ki tarah .

Yun waqt kehta hai ruk jaane ko ,
Yun waqt kehta hai faasle bhulane ko .

Yun sochti hu kya phir kabhi hamara savera aayega ?
Kya phir ye dil kabhi shor machayega ?

Sochti hu kyu na bhool jau main tumhein ya har woh baat !
Kaise maaf kru tumhe mai iss baar .

Ye jo ajeeb se faasle ho chuke hai darmiyan
Na tum ho na mai hu ab yaha !
Ye jo hum dono ke khamoshiyan hai
Kehne do inhe ..
Par shayad ab waqt aa gaya hai
Ab leti hu alvida tumse !

Kal ke savero ko jo dekhti hu mai
Nazar nhi aati hai ye raat !
Par tum dikhte nahi, un savero me mujhko..
Lagta hai savera bhi jaise ghani raat !
Kya hi kahu mai ab aur 🖋

11.

Kabhi kabhi gham ko gale lagane se gham chuth jata hai
Zindagi me Khushi aur gham dono ka apna apna hissa hai
Aur dono ke hi apne apne seekh !
Khudko kare is dard se riha , lagake isko gale !
Soche kyu aaya hai ye hisse , sikhane kya ?
Jaata hai ye aap ko banake ek behtar insan .
Isliye kyun hum kayar ki tarah isse dur bhaage
Karle zindagi ko apni isse bhi apna banake !!

12.

Kabhi kabhi shanti aur shor me antar samajh nahi aata !
Kabhi kabhi shanti me bahut shor hota hai ..
Aur kabhi kabhi bahut shor me Shanti ..!
Shayad Hume Shanti se pyar hai phir chahe voh shor me mile ya akele pan me fark nahi padta.
Aur aisi bheed ka kya fayda jaha sabke beech bhi Hume akela lage ..!
Aur aise shant rehne ka bhi kya faayda jisme ander hi ander hum ghut ghut ke reh jaaye ..!!

13.

ZINDAGI

Yun sambhalte sambhalte jab ladkhada si jaati hai kadame .
Toh kaun aata hai tumhe thaamne ?

Jab band darvajo ke peeche khaamoshi se bhari tumhaari cheekhe sunte hai tumhaare kaan
Kaun aata hai tum batau tab ??
Pyaar se tumhe behlaane !

Ye dhaagon ki silvate jab khulne si lagti hai ...
Kaun karta hai Rafu zindagi ko ?
Tum ya mai ? Ya ek aas ?

Jab tute kinaro ko silte silte tumhara dum ghut sa jaata hai ...
Zindagi me hausalo ka bhar kabhi kabhi badh sa jaata hai !

Voh aas jaise ghotatee ho tumhaare dam ko
Khushiyan jaise nochti ho jeevan ko

Kya kare zindagi ka bhar kabhi kabhi badh sa jaata hai
Kaun aata hai bolo tab thamne tumhe ?
Kon sulaata hai sirhane tumhe us berehemi si raat ?
Jab aankh band kr dekhoge toh khudko hi paaoge apne sath !
Jab tum sath do khudka .. toh dhal si jaati hai koi bhi raat .

" Hausle toote tum tootne na dena
Pankhon mein apne tum jankh lagne na dena
Yeh zindagi hai ye har mod par tumhe satayegi !
Iske nakhron se harakar
Tum kabhi dil Tod na lena ..!"

14.

ASAL MEIN KAUN HO TUM ??

Jab thakk jaate ho tum banne banane me toh asal me kaun ho tum ?
In raaston mein kaun ho tum ?

Manzilon me pahunch ke tum ho
Ya in raaston mein ho tum ?

Kabhi Kabhar kuch banne ke daud me khudko bhut piche chod aate hai hum !

Khudko khona agar paana hai
Toh phir woh kya paana hai ?
Jeevan mein toh bas yuhi chalte jaana hai ..!!

15.

WAQT

Aaj ka jo waqt hai
Kal vahi phir yaadein hongi
Waqt ki hatheli se phir
Kuch yaadein ret ki tarah ,
Haathon se fisal hi jaayengi
Un yaadon ke nagmo me se
Kuch dhun shaayad reh jaaye
Kal vaha phir aaj hoga
Aur aaj ban jaayegi
Kuch bhooli bisari yaadein

16.

SILVATIEN

Bhool ke in Andheron ko hi
Chal rahe hai tum aur mai
Ek aas ke umeed liye hi
Chal rahe hai tum aur mai
Chalo chod ke in uljhe kisso ko
Aage chal padte hai
Kal phir mil gaye kisi raah me,
Toh kar lenge is dil ke kashmakash ka zikr.
Ab zindagi aur zaya nhi karte in uljhano ko suljane me !
Aisi bhi kya uljhane ,
Ki palak jhapakte zindagi hi isme phansi ki phansi beet jaaye,
Pr suljhe na man ke ye phande !
Bhool ke Tum , mai aur hamari silvatein,
Kr dete hai khudko riha 🌟

Bahut waqt beet jata hai in silvaton ko suljhane me...
Aau hum waqt zaya nhi krte , zindagi bitane me ..!
Karte hai zindagi ek naye mod se shuru
Chod ke piche uljhe kisse puraane. !

17.

KHUDSE MOHHABAT

Is zindagi ke gamo me kaun sath deta hai? Asliyat me mayne toh Ussi vyakti ka hota hai jo apko tute huye, apne gale laga kar aap ko sambhal le .

Kyu hum ek bura Sapna samajh kar , sab bhool kar aage nhi badh paate ..?
Kyu hum bhut si cheezon ko peeche chod nhi paate ..!??

Sachme dekha jaye toh kaun rehta hai apke paas apke alawa ??
Sab toh chod hi jaate hain ..!!!
Isliye kyu kisi ke liye jagah banana ..??
Kyunki jab bhi koi aata hai !
Hum unko rakhne ke liye apni jagah khali karke unko is jagah me bhar lete hai ..!
Ab mujhe ye jagah kisi aur ko nhi dena ..!
Kyunki mere alawa koi mera sath nahi nibhaata ..!
Toh kyu mai apna waqt dusron mein zaya kru ?
Ab ye puri jagah sirf meri aur meri hai
Aur isme sirf mera haq hai !
Sach hai jab hum khud ko samajh lete hain
Aur khud ke liye khade hote hai toh aur kisi ki
Zaroorat bhi nhi hoti ..!!

Toh ab us insaan ko waqt dete hai

Jo har waqt humko thamta hai
Aur thoda apne dil ki sunte hai ..!
Aao hum khud se nazrein milate hai ..!
Khudke thode aur qareeb jaate hai
Khud ko woh pyaar dete hai
Jo befasool hi hum doosro pe lootate hai .!

18.

Zindagi ko jitna samajhte jaau ,
Ek mod me aake aisa lagne lagta hai
Jaise har cheez ke liye hum hi jimmedar hai
Pata nahi kyun aisa lagta hai
Jaise ab mujhe kuch chahiye nahi
Kyunki jitna zindagi ko samjho
Yun lagta hai jaise har pareshani
Kuch chahne se hi toh shuru hoti hai

Aur bas ek ke baad ek us se nikalne ke liye
Hum dusre preshaniyo me phaste chale jate hai
Kabhi Kabhar hum aise bhawar mein phas jaate hai
Jaha hum jo bhi kare , jidhar bhi mude
Aage Hume maat hi milegi
Pr shayad aise raston me khudko thaamna bhut zruri hota hai
Ek na ek din toh isse bahar nikalenge hum
Aur ek nayi sunehri raah haasil karenge .. !!

In raaston se hausla tod ke ,
manzilon se ruswa toh hoke nahi baith sakte
Ya raston ke kaaton ki vajah se
apni aankhon ke sapne bikhar ke
thak ke toh nahi baith sakte
hamesha ke liye ..!

19.

YAADEIN

Hum pata shor kabtak machate hai ?
Ya apne dil ki baat samjhane ki koshish tab tak karte hain
Jab tak Hume un bachi kuchi achi yaadon ke liye
Dil me umeed bachi rehti hai !
Ki chahe bura phir kitna hi kyu na ho...
Par un achi yaadon ke chalte hum khud ko us aag me phir se dhakelne ke liye taiyar ho jaate hai ..!
Chahe Hume kitni hi takleef ho in yaadon ke chalte hum baar baar khudko us aag me jhok hi aate hai
Par dheere dheere jab woh achi yaadein feeki si hojaati hain aur humaare aankhon ke samne sadharan ho jaati hai ..!
Hum uske liye ladna bhi band kr dete hai ..!
Dheere dheere achi yaadein aur buri yaadon ke Jung me achi yaadein bhut peeche chuth aati hai ..!
Aur tab hum bhi unke liye ladna band kr dete hai ..!

Takleef hoti hai
Us insaan ko apne nazron mein aise dekhne mein
Ya uska ek pal me hamara sab kuch hona aur agale hi pal kuch nhi hone me !
Us insaan ke sath har waqt betaaya hota hai
Toh lagta hai har cheez mein,
ek adhoora pan ka ehsaas humesha ke liye reh jaayega..!

Jaise kuch chut gya ho !
Par waqt dheere dheere un khali jagaho aur zakhmon ko bhar hi deta hai ..!
Aur yahi toh zindagi hai shayad ..!
Un khali jagah ko zindagi apne rango se aur apne pyaar se bhar hi deti hai .!

Aur kr deti hai
Zindagi nayi si ..!!

Silvate daag daman se chut hi jaate hai
Aur zindagi naye panne si kore kaagaz ki tarah
Phir paymaan leke aati hai
Ek nayi kahani likhne ko ..!
Aur woh bhi pehle se behtar .!

Yaadon ko kab tak hi saheja ja sakta hai
Ye zimmedari waqt ne nibhane ko de rakhi hai
Voh un panno me humesha chap jaata hai
Jo lakh toofan ke baad bhi
Sath nhi chodta
Jise zindagi apne utar chadhav se
Hata nhi pati ..!!
Jiska daaman tumse woh kabhi choda nahi paati ..!

Par kabhi kabhi kuch cheez piche chut jaati hai
Aur jo peeche chuth jaata hai voh bhut bhari hota hai
Kabhi Kabhar sahi galat ke pare ..!

Chahe jo piche chuta ho voh galat hi kyu na ho ..
dil ko bhut Khali sa kar deta hai
Kyunki galat hote huye bhi insaan kabhi kabhi
Bhut jagah bana leta hai
Bhut si yaadein hoti hai
Bhut si aise raahe hoti hai
Jisme woh insaan aapke liye khada hota hai
Aapka haath thama hota hai ..!
Mushkil hoti hai ...
Un yaadon ko apne hathon se phisalte dekhne mein
Par waqt sab waqt se theek kar hi deta hai 🍂
Ye khali jagah apne marham se bhar hi deta hai

* * *

Jitna likhungi utna hi kam hoga .
Itna hi rehne deti hu bass ab ..
Har cheez na samajh paungi na samjha paungi !
Bahut kuch hai jaanti hun !
Bhut se sawaal hai ..
Aur sabke jawaab hume abhi chahiye ..
Aur itne aawazon ke beech janti hu
Sab samajh ke bhi aisa lagta hai
Jaise sab nahi samjha hua hai
Par shayad aise hi acha hai 🍂

Kuch baaton ko waqt ke liye chod dena hi acha hota hai shayad !

Isliye phir milenge ...

Naye panno ke sath
Naye kavita aur paheliyon ke sath 🌿

***